Half A Life's History

HALF
A LIFE'S
HISTORY

ROBERT
SWARD

AYA PRESS POETRY SERIES, NUMBER FOUR

CANADIAN CATALOGUING IN PUBLICATION DATA

Sward, Robert, 1933-
    Half A Life's History

(Aya Press Poetry Series: No. 4)

ISBN 0-920544-34-7

I. Title. II. Series.

PS8587. W37H3   C811'.54   C83-098435-6
PR9199.3.S9H3

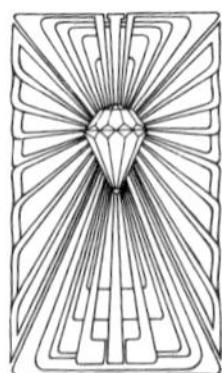

Published by Glynn Davies in May 1983 in an edition of 750 copies under the imprint of Aya Press, with the assistance of the Canada Council and the Ontario Arts Council. Typeset in Palatino by Howarth & Smith Limited (Toronto). Executed by The Porcupine's Quill, Inc. Erin.

ISBN 0-920544-34-7

For Irina and my children: Cheryl, Barbara, Michael, Hannah and Nicholas

Here I am writing to you
Half a life's history
'A horse which throws the dreamer to the ground.'
I am homesick and America has had a nervous breakdown.
I am taking shaman lessons and studying Karate.
My greatest complaint (you've offered to help) is amnesia.
Do you believe in transmigration of the soul? Yes, I do too.
But what if it can happen not only when one dies, but several times
    in an afternoon?
And I'm sure it's not properly amnesia I am speaking of.
I go out of my body, I come back in.
I say amnesia because sometimes when this happens I forget just
    who I am.
I've been doing this, I believe, with some regularity
    for a quarter of a million years. I'm doing it more and more
    frequently now because I am unhappy. Even the *light* depresses
    me — i.e., the light on Oxford Street, 6 PM on a Sunday. The
    light in Bloom's. The light in Wimpy's. I haven't seen light
    like this since the Middle Ages of the Animals.

We drink, we smoke, we go to parties. Friday night we went to
    the dullest party in 3,000 years
    in Bayswater off the Moscow Road.
I thought the whole time of algae, worms,
    primitive brachiopods, molluscs, crustaceans,
I thought of my mother and those birds with the hollow bones.
I am in the library at Swiss Cottage
    eating chocolates in the children's room.

What am I reading? Probably I have gone mad.
I am reading up on the eohippus, the first true archaic horse.
I identify. Those horses were no larger than dogs. I'm a dog
    and interested in horses that were once my own size.
Why? I don't know why. Yes, I do. It's because I feel I was
    once (also) a woolly rhinoceros.
That I am at this moment a woolly rhinoceros.
Anyway, I am no longer incapacitated by my erotic fantasies.
I am devoting my whole attention to insects, geology, etc.
Each morning I have friends come in to read me my
    biography and my passport.
Then I know who I am. Then I can pay attention to what needs
    to be done.
I go to pubs and drink and I go to the children's room at
    Swiss Cottage and read stories.
My ambition, if I stay in London, is to be a dirty old man,
    but there's too much against me.
How I long for the dark Jurassic shales
    at the foot of the Swabian Alps.

Who are these people anyway? They think they speak English,
    but I don't understand a word they say.
My only reason for coming was to learn Karate with Kanazawa,
    who has left for Germany.
Oh, I've just gone out of my body and now I'm back.
What is happening in America where, I am convinced, in my previous
    existence, I was a Confederate soldier killed in action, 186-?

Well, it doesn't matter. I'll find out soon enough and probably
    know anyway if I'd only think about it.
Before I was born, my mother who is the Mother of fire,
    gave birth to fire. Then to the Sabine women and my sister.
My father, who has an upright tail, practises and earns his living
    in Chicago. We dream alternately of the 100 elephants which
    escort the tooth of the Buddha. That he is a Rosicrucian and
    I am not is no obstacle. We have made our peace, and increasingly — .
    I might say this is a love poem for my father. A love poem for
    the 7 maidens with the heads of snakes. Half a life's history.

10

Good morning, 1860.
Good morning.
Good morning, Dr. Whimsy.
Good morning.
Good morning, Beauty.
Truth.
Queen.
Helicopter karma machine.
Industry.
Business machines. Computers.
Simplicity.
Can I have just an hour with the
    milkmaid?
I want to get back right away then to waging
    the Civil War.
What instructions are there?
Has the Queen left a note? Can I play Lord Shepperton's
    harmonica?
Women being mediums for all I know and for all
    I will ever know (How can I know that, how
    can I assign myself — ?)
I want another hour with the milkmaid and the Queen
    to read me her diaries and to instruct me
    in every extreme action of which she knows anything.
I want to know the bounds of things and sense and
    how to cleanse myself.

Is there any peanut butter?
What incredible sticky things are there to eat
    this century?
When did they invent icecream?
Anyone carrying on like this is carrying on
    for a reason.
What is the reason?
Where is the child?

But perhaps being forty years before them, I can
    become both my parents' parents.
Has that been done before?
And what if they've gone back forty or even
    sixty years?
What if they're at this moment in the process
    of becoming their own parents?
When will they get to me? When will it be my turn?
I'd like to be present and film my own birth,
To come out with a camera and to be obstetrician,
    my waiting father and Director
    at the same time.
I'd like in fact to be my mother, giving birth
    to an obstetrician-Director-my-waiting
    father and a movie camera.
And to come out with on my wrist
A wrist-sized washingmachine, etc., so I could be
    immediately fully independent. A stove. Hi-fi.
    A library. A hospital with my own
    doctors. And a complete set of in-laws.
The question most on my mind:
Where do women come from?
Women come right out of the head of the male god.
Either that or out of the earth — or things about
the earth. People here, there, everywhere, both
ears against it. Listen. Everybody. Alright,
we're listening.

Who are these women with?
Where do they come from?
How do they get that way?

The Bride is with
The Queen is with
What about Cassandra? What about Hera?
Are things complementary in more ways even
    than one suspected?
When what happens and what you do are the same thing
How is it possible to speak of loving someone or
    wasting time?

I want a banana. I want a tangerine.
I want to rim the most beautiful woman in Manhattan,
    Kansas.
What about Jesus Christ? Where is there a tape
    of Him laughing?
In sex, I've found, in loving
The discovery is the cleansing.
I want to swallow it down.
The only sadness is loving
AND NO ILLUMINATION
Beauty is wallowing.
Loving is practice.
A man having been with a woman, the woman has
    always been there
Has the man always been there?

Hello wife, hello world, hello God,
I love you; hello certain monsters,
Ghosts, office buildings, I love you. Dog,
Dog-dogs, cat, cat-cats, I love you.
Hello Things in Themselves, Things Not Quite
In Themselves (but trying), I love you.
River-rivers, flower-flowers, clouds
And sky;
          the Trolley Museum in Maine
(With real trolleys); airplanes taking
Off; airplanes not taking off; airplanes
Landing,
          I love you.

          The IRT,
BMT; the London subway
(Yes, yes, pedants, the Underground)
System; the Moscow subway system,
All subway systems except the
Chicago subway system. Ah yes,
I love you, the Chicago El-
Evated. Sexual intercourse,
Hello, hello.

Love, I love you; Death,
I love you;
        and some other things, as well,
I love you. Like what? Walt Whitman,
Wagner, Henry Miller;
            a really
Extraordinary, one-legged
Tijuana whore; I love you, *loved*
You.

        The *Reader's Digest* (their splendid,
Monthly vocabulary tests), *Life*
And *Look* . . .
        handball, volleyball, tennis;
Croquet, basketball, football, Sixty-
Nine;
        draft beer for a nickel; Women
Who will lend you money, Women
Who will not;
        Women, pregnant women;
Women who I am making pregnant;
Women who I am not making pregnant.
Women. Trees, goldfish, silverfish,
Coral fish, coral;
        I love you, I
Love you.

I did not want to be old Mr.
Garbage man, but uncle dog
Who rode sitting beside him.

Uncle dog had always looked
To me to be truck-strong
Wise-eyed, a cur-like Ford

Of a dog. I did not want
To be Mr. Garbage man because
All he had was cans to do.

Uncle dog sat there me-beside-him
Emptying nothing. Barely even
Looking from garbage side to side:

Like rich people in the backseats
Of chauffeur-cars, only shaggy
In an unwagging tall-scrawny way.

Uncle dog belonged any just where
He sat, but old Mr. Garbage man
Had to stop at everysingle can.

I thought. I did not want to be Mr.
Everybody calls them that first.
A dog is said, Dog! Or by name.

I would rather be called Rover
Than Mr. And sit like a tough
Smart mongrel beside a garbage man.

Uncle dog always went to places
Unconcerned, without no hurry.
Independent like some leashless

Toot. Honorable among scavenger
Can-picking dogs. And with a bitch
At every other can. And meat:

His for the barking. Oh, I wanted
To be uncle dog — sharp, high fox-
Eared, cur-Ford truck-faced

With his pick of the bones.
A doing, truckman's dog
And not a simple child-dog

Nor friend to man, but an uncle
Travelling, and to himself —
And a bitch at every second can.

I still heard Auntie Blue
After she did not want to come down
Again: she was skypaper, way up
Too high to pull down. The wind
Liked her a lot, and she was lots of noise
And sky on the end of the string:
And the string jumped hard all of a sudden,
And the sky never even breathed,
But was like it always was, slow and close
Far-away blue, like poor dead Uncle Blue.

Auntie Blue was gone, and I could not
Think of her face; and the string fell down
Slowly for a long time. I was afraid to pull it
Down. Auntie Blue was in the sky,
Just like God. It was not my birthday
Anymore: and everybody knew, and dug
A hole, and put a stone on it
Next to Uncle Blue's stone, and he died
Before I was even born; and it was too bad
It was so hard to pull her down; and flowers.

FROM PURDY'S IN VICTORIA, B.C.

A man dreams of searching for his Self
and finds it occupying its own private
train car. The man tells how upon hearing
his voice, his Self turns, recognizes him
and embraces him and how they walk off
closer than brothers.
                        And there you are
in Ganeshpuri, the brother I hugged
when you arrived unexpectedly
from home my final week there. My mouth
dropped open. 'Mark! What are you doing
in Ganeshpuri?'

Baba says that when we see a friend
unexpectedly in this way
and the mind stops its incessant chatter
and we draw in our breath saying, Ahhh —
in that moment of recognition
we know the pure bliss of *samadhi*.
In that moment I felt that same bliss
Seeing you in the marble courtyard.
You've outlasted me all these months
in Ganeshpuri. I laugh and wonder:
how does a man find his inner Self?
Is it possible to send a card,
write a letter or mail a Valentine
saying, 'Happy Valentine's Day, dear Self,
here is a box of the best chocolates —
from Purdy's in Victoria, B.C.'?
Is it possible to send you, dear Mark,
bright red tulips and daffodils, too
from this city of gardens
with its orange-fleshed arbutus trees,
green leaves against a blue sky,
     salt air rolling in
off the Straits of Juan de Fuca?
That's all I want to say, Brother Mark.
You've lived here, too. You know what it's like
living on this enchanted island.
Dear Brother. Dear Twin. My other Self.

HONEY BEAR

She is a Russian honey bear
With very strong soft brown arms.
Hugging her is at once a feat
Of strength and an act of gentle
        surrender.

One cannot hug the honey bear
With only half a heart. It's all
Or no honey bear. There's a snap
And vibrancy to her kisses

Pucker and snap — audible
Across a field of wild black
Berries. Honey bear loves fresh cream
And wild berries of all kinds

French cheeses and fresh homebaked bread.
She is earth tremors in the garden,
Laughter in the flower beds
Rough brown honey bear pulling weeds.

Her feet, large, perfectly
Proportioned
        are powerful as
Angel wings. A pale blue light
Surrounds her toes as she waltzes

By the clover and the mint.
Lighter than air, heavier
Than a bear. Clear-skinned lady
O fairest of the fair

BEAR MOTHER

    Mystery.
Familiarity. Moving together
of bodies. The dance of mouths,
hands, bellies and tongues lightly touching
     knees and hairs and milky toes
       *
Black bear mother with magic eyes
and dancing feet
crouching, squatting
giving birth
dropping a single cub
the cub grunting, sticky,
moaning.

Her lips are kindly and full.
Her eyes are blue,
Mouth like pale cherries
        ripe on trees
        with snow.

She appears without clothes
        or fur
In a white velvet tent
On an enchanted island.
She's a white hummingbird
At the float house
In the evening
Circling clockwise
Round the fire.
                *
Dark goes into light.
Dark is a black cord on a silver needle
Drawn by a bear
Through a cave
        shining
        glistening
In the dripping darkness
Reflecting fire.
                *
In our boat at night —
With herself as passenger —
We navigate
        over rocks,
Submerged, undiscovered islands,
Moons like gigantic human eyes,
Lunar gardens and small mansions,
Wooden houses
        floating
        in the sea.

MOVIES: LEFT TO RIGHT

The action runs left to right,
Cavalry, the waterskiers —
Then a 5-hour film, *The Sleeper*,
A man sleeping for five hours
(In fifteen sequences),
Sleeping left to right, left to right
Cavalry, a love scene, elephants.
Also the world goes left to right,
The moon and all the stars, sex too
And newspapers, catastrophe.

In bed, my wives are to my left.
I embrace them moving left to right.
I have lived my life that way,
Growing older, moving eastward —
The speedometer, the bank balance
Architecture, good music.
All that is most real moves left to right,
Declares my friend the scenarist,
Puffing on a white cigar, eating
The *Herald Tribune*, the *New Republic*.

My life is a vision, a mechanism
That runs from left to right. I have lived badly.
Waterskier, I was until recently
In the u.s. Cavalry. Following that
I played elephant to a lead by Tarzan.
Later, I appeared in a film called *The Sleeper*.
Till today, standing on the edge of things,
Falling and about to fall asking, Why?
I look back. Nowhere. Meanwhile, one or more wives
Go on stilts for the mail.

'Several *actual*, potentially and / or really traumatic situations are
depicted on these pages.'
    — *Transient Personality Reactions to Acute or Special Stress* (Chapter 5).

Photo II

The house is burning. The furniture
Is scattered on the lawn (tables, chairs
TV, refrigerator). Momma —
There is a small, superimposed white
Arrow pointing at her — is busy
Tearing out her eyes. The mute husband
(Named, arrowed) stands idly by, his hands
Upon his hips, eyes already out.
The smoke blankets the sky. And the scene,
Apart from Momma, Poppa, the flames . . .
Could be an auction. Friends, relatives
Neighbors, all stand by, reaching, fighting
For the mirrors, TV, sunglasses;
The children, the cats and speechless dogs.

SHARON CENTER, IOWA

'Some years the ground pulls harder — '

He mounts his tractor,
There are creatures in trees
Whose names I do not know.
There are others in procession before us.
Pigs the size of buffalo. Cattle
The tails and markings of horses.
Iowa. What am I doing in Iowa?
Ann lies in the sun. Dozing. Depressed.
Stripping, rising on my hind legs,
Hairy, cloven-footed,
Centaur, I declare myself / Centaur.
Then chicken. Then horse. Bull. Then pig.
She too-Centaur. Then chicken. Horse. Bull. Then pig.
Let us plant our dreams.
Write them down and plant them.
Plant sugar cubes
Make love
Then dig it up / turn it over
And plant the ground
That ground we made love on.
What will grow there?
Rhubarb.
A peach tree.
The ground holds me as I make love to it.
How is it birds no longer fly?
Horses only. The entire state of Iowa.
What about deities
These deities that eat your brains?
And why anyway should I mind that?
I am busy planting my brains.
I will harvest them remind me please before leaving.
The time has come.
O look Centaur Snowing Your eyes
Your eyes
They touch me
I have been asleep
Does it hurt?

FARMHOUSES

Climbing down from my tree, I visit my wife,
Breakfast with her, read manuscripts and shave,
I walk out of the house into a ringing
Like the ringing in my ears. It is the day —
Sunlight, pine trees, abandoned farmhouses.
I have walked again into an old landscape:
Change of direction, turnings of the mind.

ARRIVAL

The light goes out, the dark comes down,
Small cries, low murmurs of foxes.
A light descends on the trees, whitish like what
They themselves give off. Watching it, I am moved
To prayer, to the crying out of titles
Of certain poems, the names of God,
My *own* name. It takes shape before me.
It is the night's name, my wife's name.
In motion, in one another's arms,
We arrive somewhere where none of this is so.

It's all quiet and we lie here numbed.
There is motion, rough-winged barn swallows
And clouds. Butterflies loop around one another
Suggesting bows, configurations of a knot.
Both of us lose interest. The corrugated
Galvanized roof of a hundred-year-old barn
Refuses light. The sun comes off it
In unexpected intensities. The fields and hills
Form a backdrop to this. Cicadas and song sparrows.
The landscape rolls, my eyes roll with it.
Uneasily at first, unexpectedly it comes over me
That no one will ever not love here.
The new clothespins, the look of light on the line.
Old barns. Orchards. The John Deere harvester.
I am overwhelmed by the complexities
Of skunk cabbage.

     It is warmish; the breeze pleases me.
Everything is dry. We stand and walk
Around in the day. We walk out to the barn
With the corrugated top. Hours later we drink beer
And ponder the hollows under stars.
I have no thoughts whatsoever. I glance at her
And embrace her, but have nothing to say.
Implausible phrases, song titles, clichés –
     they come haltingly to mind.
Then the few convictions I have done well by.
We hold hands and walk around there.
No debts. No debts. Twelve years of manuscripts.
We can go in or out. At this moment,
For this day even, we have belonged here.
How did it happen? What have we affirmed?
We kiss the one star's lips. And always, married
               still, we move on.

HANNAH

Her third eye is strawberry jam
has a little iris in it
her eyelids
        are red
she's sleepy
        and the milk
        has gone down
        the wrong way.
I've just had breakfast
with the smallest person in the world.

BEGINNING

For days now the snow
Has been beginning.
The man has slept, has not slept;
Observes the sky. It is there
He expects the turning,
White revelations, the vision,
The difference his sleep
Has made. That time has passed,
A cloud or the falling snow.
That what has been is now
Has and has happened.

STEEPLE

The clock. Bonging away at midnight.
The moon a still, white, bent
    second hand,
— at the peak of the spire.
The sky. The face of a black
    stopped clock.

28

from 'SCARF GOBBLE WALLOW INVENTORY'

How hungry and for WHAT are the people this season
    predicting the end of the end of the end of
I've only just come home after having been away
The world sends its greetings and the greetings send
    greetings
Hello goodbye, hello goodbye
There are greetings and gifts everywhere
Children screaming and feeling slighted
The next minute we're walking along canals on the planet
    Mars
Twenty minutes later we are earthworms in black leather
    jackets, our pockets filled with hamburgers,
        Voyage to the moon.
All I am really hungry for is everything
The ability to hibernate and a red suitcase going off
    everywhere
Every cell in your body and every cell in my body is
    hungry and each has its own stomach
Are your cells eating my cells? Whose cell is the universe
    and what is it sick with, if anything?
Is the universe a womb or a mouth?
And what *is* hunger, really?
And is the end of the world to be understood in terms of
    hunger or gifts, or the tops of peoples' heads coming off?
The most complex dream I've ever dreamed I dreamed in
    London.
It involved in its entirety taking one bite of an orange

* * *

'What do you want to be when you grow up?' she says.
I'm nearly sixty.
I want to be hungry as I am now and a pediatrician.
The truth is I'm 35 and hungrier than I was when I was
    20 and a sailor.
I'm hungry for icecream made with icecream and not
    chemicals or artificial spoons
When I am 65 I want to be circumcised for the second
    time
When will the world be given a Bar-Mitzvah?
The afternoon or evening immediately following the end
    of the world.
The world's gift to us all is its ending
America can play bartender and give a little speech,
'Today I am a penis.'
That way everything can end and arrive at manhood and
    the state of buoyant madness and celebration at the
    same time
That way we don't have to have any more history but only
    food
No one has to worry about getting old
When you get fat enough or go fast enough everything
    begins happening at once
The world is where you eat and go off from into space
The end of the world is the world going off into space
Everything is happening at once and beginning to go faster
In 3000 years I don't think I've been so happy as I am
    now
The best thing that ever happened to me besides everything
    else was briefly having amnesia and enjoying it at least
    briefly
How instructive are our illnesses. How instructive is mad-
    ness and losing one's mind precisely the moment one had
    begun overvaluing that mind.
What are you waiting for? We've had the revolution.
The world is over. From now on it's every real feeling for
    itself.

If you've finished eating, I'm happy for you.
No more oral sex or oral anything.
It's peace and quiet from now on.
What a loss it is: chaos and disorder.
What one liked about chaos and disorder was chaos and
    disorder.
I'm not sure I've finished but there go my suitcases.
It's too late to change your mind.
Now the world will inspect your cells.
What did you do with all that gobble-gobble you've eaten?
And is the end of the world to be understood in terms of
    hunger or gifts (for which one is indeed grateful)
    or the tops of peoples' heads coming off?
Even now we are all saying, over and over,
I've never been so hungry in my life.
I want one more bacon-lettuce-and-tomato-sandwich,
To make love and kiss everyone I know goodbye.
Tomorrow at half past four we will all two-and-a-half
    billion of us walk slowly into orbit
If only one can do this breathing normally and not trip
    on one's breath or have stomach cramps or clammy
    hands or hysterical needs or a coughing fit or the wish to
    trample or stomp someone, but stepping peacefully
There is ALL the time in the world
There is ALL THE TIME IN THE WORLD
There is all the time in the world

We are alone, Death's thousand-year-old fiancée
And I. The thing suggests itself to me.
I step onto the front parts of her feet,
And stand like that facing her saying nothing.
In moments I lose twenty pounds and sweat. My nose
    bleeds.
It occurs to me I may never before
Have acted out of instinct. We do not embrace.
She is in her middle sixties, with varicose veins,
Whitish hair and buttocks as large as Russia.
Things come off of her in waves, merriment,
Exuberance, benevolent body lice,
Hundred-year-old blackheads. I kiss her hives.
I lick her nose that shows she drinks bottles
And bottles of Fleishmann's every day.
I am standing there in my Jewish hair
Facing her with my life. Knock, knock.
It is Death in spats and a blue business suit.
I stand there in my Jewish hair facing him.
He is very still, grinning, grayish, bemused.
Pretty soon I begin to scream. All night I scream.

Yeah. After a while I go under and kiss
Her ass. It takes a bit. Fathers and sons,
I am up to my knees in the moon.
Kiss this ghost, she says of a certain light.
I plunge my tongue into it to the ears. Madam,
I say, astounded, choking, feverish,
I have not as yet had you. Have me, she says.
Under my foreskin there is a star, whole
Constellations. Goddammit, I am not
Speaking to you here of sex! Kiss me here,
She says. Kiss me there. Stars, ghosts and sons,
                                                winged,
We are all of us winged —
                          the one thing
There is of us. Death, you old lecher,
I affirm you, I confront you with my balls;
I revere dead fish and sunken submarines,
The little red schoolhouse and the American way.
Let us in fact join hands with the universe.
Death, I have news for you; I climb into
Your young fiancée eleven times a night.
There are signs that she is pregnant.
Death, there is nothing I will not love.

They had killed Momma's brother Johnny
Nine-and-a-half times in the war.   There
Wasn't hardly anything left when
He got home: of Johnny or of Momma.
I mean he came home without his arms,
Without his ears, without his brains, or
Hair; without his loving everyone,
                              and women
That made Momma mad. He didn't like
Love no more, or Momma, and he had
Been married in between all the times
He was killed. Nine-and-a-half times!
And Momma had cried and cried and said
It was like his being killed. The Army
And President Roosevelt, General
Eisenhower . . .
                    They were all sorry,
And Momma ate the letters and the envelopes;
The telegrams, and then Johnny; the Purple
Heart, the White Heart, the gold
Star, Daddy & all of Johnny's wives.
And Momma was all that there was left.

My wife has given birth to a son, I say.
There is a five minute standing ovation.
I pass around two- and three-foot cigars,
And stand there wearied, overwhelmed with pleasure.
You can learn from no one who is not present,
Altogether in love, laughing, affirming you —
They have understood this for some time.
What is it to fly? they ask. That too is clear,
For we have all of us taken hands,
Reverentially, and are in flight
In and out of classrooms, down the halls, out
The windows, over football fields, tennis courts,
The thing happening, out of hand,
Let it go —
Ascension, commitment, perfection, love.

Another thing that glows, is dogs.
We had this dog, Eugene,
        that glowed.
It struck you at once, 'That dog glows!'
That was the way people put it.
That was the way it was.
The whole dog glowed.
You shut your eyes, and still you knew it.
The dog glowed. And did not mind itself.
Went on like that —
People cried. I cried. Even my father
        and mother cried.
The dog did that.

Then they'd all begin too,
To glow
And go away
But not to not glow.

And they were the same people in my dreams.
The same people. The same dreams.

Always, and I am there too. And
All other things,
When there are people,
And when there are not.

        And
I have no resignations to tender.

All over newspapers have stopped appearing,
And combatants everywhere are returning home.
No one knows what is happening.
The generals are on long distance with the President,
A former feature writer for the New York Times.
No one knows even who has died, or how,
Or who won last night, anything.
Those in attendance on them may,
For all we know, still be there.
A few speak compulsively, telling too much,
Having sat asleep in easy chairs.

All over newspapers have stopped appearing.
Words once more, more than ever,
Have begun to matter. And people are writing
Poetry. Opposing regiments, declares a friend of mine,
Are refusing evacuation, are engaged instead
In sonnet sequences; though they understand, he says,
The futility of iambics in the modern world.
That they are concerned with the history and meaning
Of prosody. That they persist in their exercises
With great humility and reverence.

DREAMS

For John Wayne

Everything costs. The Revolution, featuring dreams
                   the quality of light in Aspen, Colorado
                   the visit here recently of John Wayne

I woke this morning and was scratching.
Have I become an apologist for some quaint aesthetic?
How is it 7 years ago, when I was first advised of Insurrection
My thoughts were all of metre and the New Criticism?
At heart, I tell myself, I am an arsonist.
Yet last evening in the firehouse I was reading aloud

                   from the Selected Poems
                   of Benito Mussolini
                   Hitler's Sonnets

And then later at Guido's playing tapes
Of Lyndon Johnson reading Homer

There are gulls on the Riviera sipping gin and tonic.
Every third icecube is filled with tissues of the brains
Of murdered American dinosaurs.

Senator Hickenlooper, I will buy you an apocalypse.
Do you want a red apocalypse, or a green apocalypse?
Would you like it seasoned with marijuana
Or oregano?
All night in the mountains old men with chainsaws
Are cutting their way to the moon.

Senator, let us order an investigation.
That the sun has risen.
Seven times in one day.
I am on a ski lift on my way to the moon.
Hand-in-hand with the moon,
The astronauts with chainsaws,
Firechief in my arms,
I am scratching and falling.
All my poems are burning.
And the cities are burning.
There are learned gentlemen making inventories,
There are others on their knees sucking them off.
Everyone is occupied.
I am feeling depressed,
        idle
        a little stupid.

What will be / the unimaginable
It turns out
Is only what we have been waiting for,
Dinosaurs minotaurs eating the moon's genitals,
The sun in revolt,
        starting over.

                * * *

The light
The rain

Rocks know what the rocks say
Fire speaking with the wind

Three times the light and then the light the Sky changes

What is it flows past stars?
Birds not flying but hopping over trees.
The writing. On pomegranates.
The word *snail*, the word for rain wizard
Butterfly
Word for the first time.
Lovers as they read. Hair wrist neck as he tastes
Her ears. Rock light the water stars

I walk downhill on my hands
The wind rising,
        the hulls of ships
    which way
Which way to the Revolution?

Pine cones, aspen,
Starlight, the light
World one way, then another
The light rising,
The light drawn up into stars

Voice is light,
The world is light
The stars, their hands
Striking through

      * * *

The day is clear.
Cypresses, like giant birds, are circling above us.
They are silent, can see for miles,
Are moving eastward.
With them are flying Hawthorns,
Sumac, Persian Walnuts.
Great hawks and the moon
Are in formation behind them.

> 'And he was clothed with a vesture dipped in blood:
> and his name is called The Word of God . . . the sword
> proceeded out of his mouth.'
>   (Revelation 19: 13-21)

You are being overthrown,
That valley to the east,
The stars that have fallen
There,
The wind that is rising,
These things must be attended to.
That valley is plotting against you,
The stars are against you.
The light, that light off those mountains,
That light is against you.
You turn away,
You hear nothing.
The world is rising,
The rocks are against you.
Those stars, that plain,
That city you have never seen,
Whose name you do not know,
That city is against you,
Is rising with the bare plain
Against you.

You turn away,
Your astronomers, mystics, schoolchildren,
Are in revolt.
All your pekingese and goldfish
Have escaped.
The grass is burning.
There are volcanoes in Missouri.

All your pine cones,
Your orange blossoms
Are in flames;
Moths peering in at your windows,
Meteors, comets
Particles of sand, the cosmic dust . . .

You turn away.
Have noticed nothing.
The lovers
Rising against you, You
Have not noticed,
What else remains?
Walk now. Take yes one giant step.

For John Torres

The thing is not to conserve mass, he says,
But to release form. The figure,
It is space makes it, granite now, it
Is another figure. Crystal / grains,
Odd quirks, flaws to be made life of.
Eyes walk into it, led by details.
Is there, they ask, a way out? The way In.

NIGHTGOWN, WIFE'S GOWN

Where do people go when they go to sleep?
I envy them. I want to go there too.
I am outside of them, married to them.
Nightgown, wife's gown, women that you look at,
Beside them — I knock on their shoulder blades
Ask to be let in. It is forbidden.
But you're my wife, I say. There is no reply.
Arms around her, I caress her wings.

BARBECUE

They were spraying Pepsi and moth-juice
On the fire. The mosquitoes, lawn-flies
And moths dove, flashed and were painlessly
Consumed. There was applause
                              . . . we entered.
And while my wife was kissed, they clapped
Me on the back. They wanted to know
That I was there; and then I kissed them
Down their throats, choked and knew that they were there.

And after I had kissed those who had
Kissed my wife, and after they kissed me,
We sprayed one another, scratched and dove
After the moths. We flashed, painlessly,
And emerged to munch the ashes, coals
To sip moth-juice, lemon juice and gin.
And (again) we clapped one another
Laughed, kissed, sipped, puffed and swallowed cigarettes.

II

When the Ginns arrived, they were pounded
On their backs. Our fists came out their mouths
(We all took turns laughing hands that way,
And toasting with one another.)
                              Poor
Wrist-throated Mrs. G.! She was mad.
Her breasts were ferocious olives. She
Wouldn't smile, or sip — and we all
Took turns mixing drinks through her (and Mr. G.)

45

III

The cat-girl would not believe in it
And crouched there pained, purring with the pups;
(Their tails were remarkably alike
And neither pronounced upon events
With them.) From time to time they'd lick one
Another, or the cream-dip, but otherwise
Were still
               . . . though one of the pups had tried
The fire, and the cat-girl
               sleekly swallowed gin.

IV

Someone found Lil, the wife of no one,
Buried beside the spit. She wanted
A martini; we obliged, and then
Reburied her.
                    Fran nibbled at the
Charcoal in Bernie's fingernails.
                              They'd
Expelled her from Home Economics.

And Bernie dove in after the moths
Only to be buried, topped, beside the spit.

V

The sky was rainbow strips of chrome, clouds
And the sun, the great, archetypal
Ford: pork-sauced and on the suburban
Spit of heaven.
                    And Lil's angel waved
Free, fulfilled and married now, to chrome
. . . sipping gin and tonic.
                    We all stared,
Climbed upon our spit, and then dove
In after the moths.
                    — The fire attained to Lil.

Unfortunately, the rest of us
Did not. And we had to try to tell
(Again) whether or not we were there.

The fire was a Ford, without chrome, pure
As gin, as cream-dip, moths or spray, death
And we sang to it: its attaining
To heaven, to Lil, to space, ourselves
And the archetypal Ford.
                    The Ford honked, then

Backed off its spit, and began to set.
In the other distance, in the space
The consuming that is east, the night
Beyond where the moths take form, beyond
What we flash for when we die,
                         we sense
The white-walled dawn, time and tomorrow's
Ford.
          The cat-girl vomited, and there was Mars,
The suburban star of barbecue.

47

VI

The party had somehow failed. The cards —
And there was Rummy, large as Lil, four'd
The evening star. It was time for gin
And time for light!
                    No one would admit
That he was there; we hid in front of
One another's wife. The women hid

Beside the flames — the way they flickered
Through their eyes. I kept trying to put my tongue

Into their cards, into their eyes, ears
Throats, between their teeth; but theirs were there

Between mine. I bit them. And they cried
With half their tongues
                        munching diamonds and spades.

And the bushes had begun the moon,
Ending 'gin', martinis and marriage.

Suddenly the women screamed. The moon
Burst through, revealing their husbands, the pup-girl

Themselves. The bushes became the lawn;
The night, the earth; and the moths, the sun.

The men became their wives; and the wives
Became the men, for the most part re-

Marrying themselves. The men were asleep
Beside their wives, smiling, spitted, still

Illicit. — Morning. My wife and I
Sipped gin; I was Bernie, and she the moths.

MOTHERS-IN-LAW

Married twice now, I've had two
Mothers-in-law. One visited us
And required, upon departure,
The services of three gentlemen
        with shoehorns
To get her back into her large black
Studebaker.

        The other, Momma-law the Present,
Is (with the exclusion neither
        of that other,
        my wives
        nor the fathers-in-law
        of either marriage),
That Studebaker.

PET SHOP

The hundred dollar cats, the thousand
Dollar dogs; the lions, the tigers;
The six miniature, white, snake-eating
Fish; the snakes, the monkeys (with grins like
Gelded poodles); the parakeets; owls
Flamingos, pink pigeons and the small, headless
Proprietor, silky, creeping and jeweled.

49

Saanichton, B.C.

Scarlet perches on the office windowsill
shrieking, hollering, barking

Like a dog. She knocks her mottled beak
against the warehouse window

And tries to open
the metal hook and eye latch.

There are parrot droppings
on the telephone and Scarlet has eaten

Part of the plastic receiver.
The parrot slides like a red fireman

With yellow and blue feathers
up and down the cord,
        holding on

With her beak, maneuvering gracefully
        with her claws.
When I approach she calls, 'Hello, hello . . .'

Walks up my trouser leg holding on
with her macaw's beak. I feed the bird

Oranges and pears, almonds
and sunflower seeds.

I swivel my head round and round
in imitation of her neck movements.

'What's happening?' she asks,
and again, 'What's happening?'

'Hello, cookie. Yoo-hoo . . .
Can you talk, can you talk?' she asks

Chewing for several minutes,
finally swallowing
      a leather button

Off my green corduroy jacket, threatening,
ready to tear my ear off,

Biting if I place my finger
in her mouth. Her tongue is black

And her beady eyes piercing like an eagle's.
She wants a response, tests my reactions.

Tenderly the parrot walks up my corduroy jacket,
sensually restraining her claws. I'm aroused.

When a dog barks, she barks too: Rrf, rrf.
Casually, a relaxed but authentic

Imitation. 'Hello darling,' she breathes,
looking me in the eye knowing I know

If it pleases her she might bite my ear off.
'Yoo-hoo, yoo-hoo, now you say something,' she says.

Sonnet

Of Love, my friends (after such sophistry
And praise as yours), may one presume? Well, then,
Let me begin by begging Agathon:
Good sir, is not your love a love for me?
And *not* a love for those who disagree?
Yes, true! And what is it that Love, again,
Is the love of? Speak! It is the love again
Of 'Socrates.' Love, then, and the Good, are me.

Explain! Is Love the love of something, or
The love of nothing? Something! Very true.
And Love desires the thing it loves. Right.
Is it, then, really me whom you adore?
Or is it nothing? O Socrates, it's you!
Then I am Good, and I am yours. Agreed!

She lies upon a tawny mat
Of effluence — and leopard spots.

And he (*he's hers*
and she knows it!)

Can but barely be seen, crouched
and to the left of her.

One ear, an eyebrow, and a bit of cheek
are all that show of him.

The caption (again) suggests that it is fun
(*fabulous fun*) being female

At a time like this! And, indeed,
it looks like fun.

Her eyes are huge and subtly closed
as leopard spots; and her lips are spread.

She is, in fact, a deodored leopardess
about to take the male.

But again, the caption: *You are the very air*
he breathes (the male is hard upon her).

She appears to be undisturbed by this;
and with both shaved armpits bared, she arches

For him. One is inclined to think of her
as being altogether without fear; she smiles,

And takes the male. Neither deodorant,
no effluence, could do more.
                              She smiles,
and she lies there, the very air
he breathed.

This, O my stomach, is a painting
Of the Civil War. Look — Antietam.
All over there are dead,
Noble Northern, Noble Southern, dead.
One, no, no, several wear beards:
They are all General Ulysses S. Grant
      beards,
Noble, truly noble beards.
The Union Side, O my soul, see them!
All, all of them noble,
All, all of them waving,
Resembling, bearing the name
Walt Whitman. They are all on horseback,
All with maps and swords, banners
And copies of last Sunday's
New York Times Book Review;
Watching through binoculars,
Writing letters, keeping journals,
Reading *Leaves of Grass* . . .

And there is Barbara Frietchie.
Hi, Barbara. Barbara's pregnant.
She is soon to be the mother
Of Abraham Lincoln, Dr. Oliver Wendell Holmes
And Carl Sandburg.

This is an historical moment;
Very historical. You can feel it
And read about it, too
(And General Stonewall Jackson,
Clare Boothe Luce, Robert E. Lee
        and many others),
In AMERICAN HERITAGE,
Edited by Bruce Catton,
With whose kind permission
I herewith reprint this painting.

                * * *

Song: 'There's No War Like Civil War'

        O, the Civil War's
        The only war,
        The only way, the only war;
        The finest war,
        Yes, the noblest most unforeign war,
        The finest only noblest most
        Unforeign war
        That ever I did see.   (Chorus, etc.)

We are in Chicago's Waldheim cemetery.
I am walking with my father.
My nose, my eyes,
    left pink wrinkled oversize
       ear
My whole face is in my armpit.

We are at the stone beneath which lies
My father's mother;
There is embedded in it a pearl-shaped portrait.
I do not know this woman.
      I never saw her.
I am suddenly enraged, indignant.
I clench my fists; I would like to strike her.
My father weeps.
He is Russian; he weeps with
    conviction, sincerity, enthusiasm.
I am attentive.
I stand there listening beside him.
After a while, a little bored,
     but moved,
I decide myself to make the effort;
I have paid strict attention;
I have listened carefully.
Now, I too will attempt tears;
      they are like song.
      they are like flight.
I fail.

I am downtown. I am wearing sunglasses,
    phony nose,
And big inch-and-a-half-long
    false teeth;
I have them jammed on over
My other teeth.
I have the look of unabashed stupidity.
People comment on it.
Some hoodlums jeer at me,
    throw rocks at me.

It is raining. Also, it is snowing.
There are carols. It is December,
    late December,
Nearly Christmas.

Old men and women are huddled in the corridor
Of the Chicago Public Library.
I go there and huddle too.
I keep on my sunglasses and nose.
People like them. They admire them.
Then they look at me. They look closely,
And huddle against me. They pick my pockets,
    my pubescent blackheads,
My father's watch chain.
One of them, a dwarf, takes me by the hand.
We go walking, just the two of us.
After a while, we begin to fly;
We fly very slowly and low
And toward the Lake. And then back.

I fall asleep. I have bad dreams;
I awaken —
Waldheim Jewish Cemetery,
The Outer Drive,
Stainless steel florist shops,
The traffic lights,
Red, amber and green.

I enter off Montrose Avenue.
Slowly, slowly
I begin the long swim
   to Michigan.

By the swimming
The sand was wetter
The farther down you dug; I dug:
My head and ear on top
Of the sand, my hand felt water . . .
And the lake was blue not watching.
The water was just waiting there
In the sand, like a private lake.
And no one could kick sand
Into my digging, and the water
Kept going through my fingers slow
Like the sand, and the sand was water too.
And then the wind was blowing everyplace,
And the sand smelled like the lake,
Only wetter. It was raining then:
Everybody was making waxpaper noises,
And sandwiches, kicking sand
And running with newspapers on their heads;
Baldmen and bathinghat-ladies, and naked people.
And all the sand turned brown and stuck together
Hard: and the sky was lightning, and the sun
Looked down sometimes to see how dark it was
And to make sure the moon wasn't there.
And then we were running: and everybody was under
The hotdog-tent eating things, spitting very mad
And waiting for the sky, and to go home.

For Hannah and Sky

The lagoon goon
hair like spaghetti, like blue metal, like wet Brillo
eyes like alphabet soup
teeth like disintegrating wood
ears like old tires
belly button like a peanut tube
legs like string beans
butterfingers
no arms
but wings like lettuce leaves
one giant foot that has nine toes
nose like an armpit
a tongue like a horseshoe
and if it sticks its tongue out at you
it's good luck.

Three-toed, one-headed, its wings the size
Of chicken-feet — and largest (next to
The ostrich) of all existing birds . . .
The emu stands, colossal, ratite
Six feet high
                         its god enplumaged, dark
Hidden in the dismal, drooping, soft
Brown hair.
                    Its hips, hump, its bulge, perhaps
Of flightlessness, or sky — appear as speed;
The stunted cause, the befeathered, round
Sloping, still embodiment of speed.

The emu runs, swoop-skims, a two-shanked
One-humped, egg-hatched camel: the bird most
Like a camel.
                    Avoiding deserts
However, the emu inhabits
Open fields and forests where, keeping
In small companies, it feeds on fruit
(Of the emu tree), herbage and roots . . .
Now and then booming, with subsequent,
And peculiarly hurried efforts,
At breeding.
                    Extinct, in Tasmania
On Kangaroo, King and Wing Islands,
The bird is found, and in small numbers,
In Southeastern Australia.
                         IT BREEDS
Its nest, as if it had been rolled in
And humped (in reverse), is a shallow
Sandy, green-egg-filled pit, the eggs of which, all
Nine (to thirteen), are incubated
By the cock, an earnest, familial
Type of ostrich.

          The young, at birth, bear thin
Length-striped down, are wattleless, and walk;
Cursëd, crane-necked, blank, dull adult-eyed
Baby, camel, ostrich-ducks . . . in file
Swift, point-beaked,

               mothered, three-toed, one-headed
— an image, but for the stripes (and down),
Of itself, in age.

          Its booming note, god
And size, are at rest in it, in its
Conspicuous state of egglessness.
It screams, booms, bounds

          . . . BECOMES IMMENSE, FLIES
Extinct, shaggy, stripeless (in age)

               FLOATS
Its head in the camel clouds, the hump
The bulge, the sandlessness that is God.

Song is not singing,
        the snow

Dance is dancing,
         my love

On my knees, with voice
      I kiss her knees

And dance; my words are song,
        for her

I dance; I give up my words,
     learn wings instead

We fly like trees
      when they fly

To the moon. There, there are
        some now

The clouds opening, as you, as we
       are there

            Come in!

I love you, kiss your knees
        with words,

Enter you, your eyes
        your lips, like

           Lover

Of us all,

        words sweet words,
        learn wings instead.

The trees bend, the colors run —
Reds into yellow, greens,
                              grays
Into white.
                    The bark, birch-bark,
Slips from its tree;
                    September,
(Wet leaves, the sun falling still,
Compost,
                    the hush of things burning,
      birdsong . . .)
                    pine trees
      white, white night light
Steaming, all cool in a mist.

from: TORONTO ISLAND SUITE

I used to live in Victoria, B.C., the whitest city on the greenest island under the bluest sky in Canada, Victoria, the Miami Beach of Canada, where gentle, 100-year-old Englishmen and Victorian alligator matrons hold formal tea parties at which the pre-recorded dialogue is broadcast from soggy, transistorized, imported tea bags and the participants only move their lips and the encouraging concepts proceeding from the teapots bear the unmistakable ring, rhythm and rhyme of Rudyard Kipling.

But now I live near the grayest city under the most shifting, rainy, summery, muddy, cloudless, overcast, Lakey sky, and on an even more enchanted, more emerald-like island, rock-hard, iron-cold in glacial winter, sandy, soft and welcoming in summer, and to which alien, burly sheriffs with jutting, Metro Parks bulldozer chins to which eviction notices are pinned, descend growling 'Knock, knock, let me come in,' and 600 determined hobbits, linking arms, reply, singing:

> Sheriff man, sheriff man
> Wolf at the door;
> Sheriff man, sheriff man
> Don't step on the floor.
>
> Sheriff man, sheriff man
> Jawbone at the door,
> Sheriff man, sheriff man
> Don't come back no more.

'Yep, bulk garbage day on the Island is something special.
You know, there's a nobility to junk. It's already been loved
once, at least. And it's not trying to seduce you into buying
it. There's a nobility in the fact the garbage is *not* asking you
to buy it.

'What is bulk garbage day?' I ask with some scepticism,
wondering if I'm being put on.

'Ah, you're new here, that's right. Well, on the 15th of
April and again in May everyone throws out all the junk
they've been saving through the winter. The things that are
too big or bulky to put out with the regular garbage. You'll
find broken fishing rods, rusty old motors and really useful
things like slightly damaged socket wrenches and bolt
busters.

'You'll find these things resting on a throne of green gar-
bage bags filled with leaves — that the Islanders have put
against the base of their houses for insulation.

'Bulk garbage day has to do with potential. You feel a kind
of intensity as you go through all that garbage. There's a
certain excitement picking up all sorts of objects you may
not need. And there's an element of chance. Surprises.
God, you see crazy combinations of things: asphalt shingles
and bicycle tires. Old chesterfields and electric motors.

'June and July bulk garbage days are less significant than
April and May 15th. That's because when spring arrives
you have this natural opening of the pores. April in Toronto
is cleansing time.'

'Sounds like a mass sauna bath where hundreds of people
open their pores and secrete busted and rusty stove pipes
and Christmas toys from Honest Ed's instead of sweat.'

'Right. But there's a dignity, a respect for those objects. As
I say, Islanders tend to place their busted radios, wrecked
toys and things on a throne of garbage bags. That's because
they have some affection for what they're throwing out.
And that's the point, that's what bulk garbage day is all
about; the nobility of junk.

I asked a nine-year-old girl who has lived here all her life
what things she liked most about the Islands and she
answered by writing a six-line poem:

Walking The Pier At The Eastern Gap

Sunrise on the gap
Looking into the clear water when the sun is hot
Fishing in the pond
Catching crayfish with a worm
Chasing the ships that race by
Walking along at night.

— Sky Dasey, Age 9

*

Islands of squat cozy homes,
'where there's no chocolate
and it's quiet,'
says my nine-year-old.
Where parishoners and their children
once skied to church,
St. Andrew-on-the-Lake,
And where, in a community of 700 people,
it is possible to know
every man, woman and child,
and every cat and dog, by sight
if not by name.
And where a child laughs, 'The Islands
are like one big family. Everyone
knows everyone. The hardest part
is the boat. Getting to the ferry docks
on time. You have to adjust,' she says.

'But best of all is the people.
You know Percy, the milkman? Everyone
knows Percy. He's been here for years.
He lets me pay forty cents for the yoghurt
instead of forty-five. There's some great people
over here. Like septic Sam who used to pump
the septic tanks.

'Yeah, and I knew a painter. He wrapped his house in alu-
minum foil to reflect away bad vibrations. And one day he
burned all his paintings on the beach. But he was a good
painter. I mean, really. He used to wear wrap-around sun-
glasses and a turban with a whole lot of different colours for
each day in the week. Monday he'd wear one colour. Tues-
day he'd wear another colour. Even for the Islands he was
pretty astounding for his time. He had a thing about elec-
tricity. He cooked all his meals in a Campbell soup can over
a candle because he didn't want to use electricity.

'I knew a preacher, too. He wasn't a real preacher. He'd just
dress up like one. Once I saw him dressed up in a Union
Jack. And then one day, no one knows why, he just left. He
left dinner on the stove, my Mom says, food in the fridge,
clothes in the closet. He went away and never came back.
He lived in that little white house . . .

'And there's my mother's friend who uses bird calls to call
her children. That's nothing. One mother has a conch. And
another uses a bell to call her kids.

'And I know a lady who puts out the garbage in the alto-
gether. There's always somebody nude sunbathing in her
yard there.

'Did you know there was a Celtic Island, St. Brendan's,
which was a soul kingdom?' she asks. 'St. Brendan's Island
even turns up on maps of 17th Century Ireland. What if Al-
gonquin and Ward's were the dwelling place of the spirit,
the soul kingdom for the City of Toronto? Why would
Metro Toronto want to destroy its soul-kingdom?

    *

. . . and what is this place anyway?
sandpit, sand pile
sand bar
ground up pieces of the Ice Age,
rocks and marsh,
eroded sandstone washed over
from the Scarborough Bluffs
by the action of the 'currents of water
rebounding from Niagara Falls.'
Ten thousand years of sediment.
Clay, sand, gravel and boulders.
Spring floods and winter storms.
We live on a melted glacier.
Enormous fields of ice moving
slowly
   down mountain slopes,
across valleys
   spreading outward,
ice travelling one to two feet
a day,
   grinding, pushing along
whole chunks of the frozen world,
a moving, perennial snowfield
finally dissolving
   Ice Age ten thousand years ago.

The waters slowly recede.
Islands appearing like the dark, wrinkled crown
    of an infant's head
    as it emerges,
body still in the body
of the mother, the mother
bearing down,
    pushing out,
Islands being born out of the Lake,
increasing in size
    a few inches each year.
The shoreline moving outward,
    changing
    with every storm.

        'I know this is a soul kingdom because if it
        were not a soul kingdom there would not be
        so many species of birds here.'

On Mugg's Island
at the bird sanctuary
are mallards and grackles and wrens,
blackcrowned night herons,
and territorial Canadian geese
who attack visitors
who dare to trespass too near
their nests. Honking and barking,
the bird spreads its wings
and punches the intruder
smack in the head and with
sufficient strength
to knock him over.
And ruby-throated hummingbirds
with their iridescent throats,
the smallest bird in Canada.

And the snow goose
with its highpitched monosyllabic
KWOK KWOK
its black wing tips and pinkish bill
flying north night and day without stopping.
flying to Mugg's Island from Maryland
heading for the Arctic,
snow goose
taking one mate,
one nesting ground for life.

                    *

A friend writes of how
'the eighty-year-old houses
have acquired a permanent smile,
their corners lifted into lopsided grins
cradled as they are
by the roots
of close-standing
willow and cottonwood trees.'

Island houses that began
as simple canvas tents
set on raised wooden platforms,
the platforms
    mounted on rocks
or positioned squarely on the ground.
A screened porch for sleeping,
a canvas-covered kitchen
and the space between,
an open air livingroom.

Permanency comes
with installation of walls
and a tarpaper
or shingled roof.
Eighty years later,
roofs buckle and bulge,
sloping in all directions.

71

'Albrecht Schoenborn, 74, who has lived on the Islands since
he and his family arrived in Metro after World War II, won-
dered if Ontario action would mean he'll be able to spend at
least another summer tending his garden and making pot-
tery in the shed behind his Algonquin Island home.

'At least it's a stay of execution,' he said, sitting in his back-
yard sorting pottery as his wife Luise picked lettuce from
the garden and a hummingbird hovered near some
raspberry canes.

Old black-and-white-faced squaw ducks
come down from the arctic to winter here,
with ptarmigan, bufflehead and snowy owls
who can be seen on frigid nights huddling
against the lights at the Island airport.

When the Island warms, five-petalled
blue-eyed grass appears, and the hermit thrush,
up from Carolina, dazzles everyone as
it sounds two notes at the same time.

Out on the boardwalk, singing beyond
the dogwood shrubs, the lilac, the forsythia,
the willow and the white bridal wreath,
Elizabeth sews baby's breath
and dried cornflowers onto a kite,
blue and green ribbons making up its tail.
Kites: kites with streamers,
6 by 5 foot kites, decorated with red feathers,
gliders and flying machines, and diamond-shaped
clear plastic 12-foot delta-winged ripstock nylon,
cloth and paper kites.

When the geese go by, they nod, and the old squaw ducks
and the snow goose and the hermit thrush sing for her,
as do the gadwalls, blue-winged teals, the coots,
the wood ducks and the red-breasted merganser.

Edward 'Ned' Hanlan, 1855-1908

A boat was his baby carriage,
this 'young phenom'
    as the gamblers called him,
prodigy who, at 5, rowed
    across Toronto Bay.
'Unreserved, gracious, kindly
    and clean,'
said the newspapers.
Hanlan, the rowing innovator,
    'father of the sliding seat,'
winner of 300 consecutive races.
Part-time bootlegger,
    competent eluder of the police —
'Hanlan jumped into a skiff and started
rowing furiously . . .'

Hanlan who, during a race,
    would actually stop rowing
and allow the competition to creep up
    even with his stern
'and then accelerate.'
Hanlan, whose style was one of effortlessness
    and apparent ease,
who, typically, 'won as he liked.'

And the band struck up 'See The
    Conquering Hero Comes'
as, aboard the S.S. *City of Toronto*,
    he returned from the great
    Schuylkill River Regatta
having defeated the two Americans, Fred Plaisted
    and Pat Luther.
'This fine young Irish lad'
whose Hotel Hanlan
was closed down
    by licensing authorities,
'headstrong Hanlan,' some called him,
    upstart idol of Toronto.
Hanlan who, during regattas,
    would kiss his hand three times to the crowd
and then resume rowing.

I wrote for myself
for people. I've
changed.
I've changed since I
began writing *I write*
for myself. I believe
more than ever in
music, in the sound,
however gotten, of music
in people's poetry. Rhyme
more than ever. Talk
people talking, getting that
into one's poetry that
is my poetics. Love
hate lies laughing stealings
self-confession, self-destruction
get them all get
them all down.
No one has to
read them. No one
has to publish them.
I am more and
more for unpublished poetry.
That is why I
have a pseudonom that
is why I now
publish poetry. To control
the view.
To hell with the Business
of Anthologies. To hell
with Anthologies.

To hell too with the way I
taught poetry in the
1950s, 60s and 70s.
One way and another
I have written angry poetry for
twenty years. Now I
want music only and
the sounds of people.
I want poems
that sing
and can use
the word heart and
self-confession and incorrect
grammar and the soils
and stains of Neruda
and Lorca and Kabir
and Williams and
Whitman and Yeats.

Forty-four years old.
Stands on his head
ten minutes daily morning
breakfast, supper.
Writing less and less.
Evaporating into the air
feet first. I won't
ever die. I'll simply
stand on my head
and disappear into the
air just like that.

I don't believe in
imagination. The prairies
as a landscape
are imagination. Just as
England is, as a landscape,
a failure of imagination.

Africa is imagination. India
is reaching even further
than that. And that
is why I will
go to India which
I will in seven
days time. So this
is a time capsule
in case anyone is
interested and in case
I never come back.
This is a
statement of poetics written
as 'Goodbye to myself.'

   Goodbye for
   now, goodbye
   goodbye goodbye
   to myself,
   goodbye goodbye
   for now
   goodbye myself,
   goodbye for
   now goodbye.

ACKNOWLEDGMENTS

Grateful acknowledgment is made to the editors of the following publications for permission to reprint many of the poems in this book: *Transatlantic Review* (London), *The Chicago Review, The New Orleans Poetry Journal, Poetry* (Chicago), *Fiddlehead* (New Brunswick), *Approach, Epoch* (Ithaca, N.Y.), *Mount Shasta Selections, Ambit* (London), *The Greenfield Review, The Chelsea Review* (New York), *The Hudson Review, Choice* (Chicago), *The New Yorker, From A Window* (Tucson, Arizona), *Carleton Miscellany, Arts in Society* (Madison, Wisconsin), *Tuatara* (Victoria, B.C.), *Malahat Review* (Victoria, B.C.), *Prism International* (Vancouver, B.C.), *Toronto Life, Poetry Toronto, New: American & Canadian Poetry, El Corno Emplumado* (Mexico City), *Extensions* (New York), *Kayak #21* (San Francisco). Some of these poems have been recorded by Western Michigan University's Aural Press (1005) and the Library of Congress. Others have appeared in the following anthologies: *New Yorker Book of Poems; Oxford Book of Light Verse; Penquin Book of Animal Poetry; The Voice That is Great Within Us; A Controversy of Poets; To Say The Least: Canadian Poets From A to Z; The Treasure of Our Tongue; Inventions For Imaginative Thinking; Sports Poems; Neue Amerikanische Szene* (Joseph Melzer Verlag, Germany); *The Now Voices; Inside Outer Space; The Practical Imagination* and others. R.D. Brinkmann and Peter Behrens have translated some of these poems into German in a volume titled *Silver Screen, Neue Amerikanische Lyrik,* Kiepenheuer & Witsch, Köln. Others have been translated into Spanish by Madela Ezcurra and Eduwardo Costa and appeared in *Airon* 9, Buenos Aires, Argentina. Portions of *Horgbortom Stringbottom* were translated into French and read on Radio Canada's CBUF-FM by Dr. Olivier M. Abrioux. Some of the poems in this collection previously appeared in *Advertisements,* Odyssey Chapbook Publications (Chicago); *Uncle Dog & Other Poems,* Putnam & Co., Ltd., London; *Kissing The Dancer,* Cornell University Press, Ithaca, N.Y. *Thousand-Year-Old Fiancée;* Cornell University Press; *Horgbortom Stringbottom, I Am Yours, You Are History,* Swallow Press, Chicago; *The Iowa Poems,* Stone Wall Press, Iowa City, Iowa; *The Jurassic Shales,* Coach House Press, Toronto and *Honey Bear on Lasqueti Island,* B.C., Soft Press, Victoria, B.C.

I wish to thank the Canada Council, the Corporation of Yaddo and the Edward MacDowell Association for affording me an opportunity to complete this book.